D1457848

10/6
Direct (A.E.Dodd)

WEAVER HILLS

and other Poems

WEAVER HILLS

AND OTHER POEMS

by

A. E. DODD

THE FORTUNE PRESS
15 BELGRAVE ROAD, LONDON, S.W.I

© A. E. DODD 1967

FIRST PUBLISHED 1967

MADE AND PRINTED IN GREAT BRITAIN

CONTENTS

CONTENTS—*Continued*

WEAVER HILLS

Clarity unrolls a map of many shires :
Quiet village—Wootton, Ellastone—
Beyond them hill and woodland, wells of shade,
Mown meadow, pasture, green and different green ;
West, against the sun, like dolphins from the sea,
Rise Wrekin, Breidden, Wenlock Edge ;
East, clear brilliance, limestone low, tree-clumped,
Hiding the well-known Dale ;
From the furthest valley south, Lichfield—
Three spires, faint but unmistakable,
Built consciously to raise the mind.

But those other clusters of fat bobbin towers?
Groups of steaming funnels, concrete white?

They mark the valley line of industry
And power, riveting the mind to brain . . . to earth :
Easy for the medieval smith,
Down in the village there, to forge hot iron
In links around his little world,
From the same billet a horse's shoe,
His neighbour's mattock and his church's sconce ;
Earthly power was known, muscle, water, wind,
Limited—the source of power, fulcrum,
Object moved all seen together, set within
The finite framework of unquestioned creed.
Nearer in time the village carpenter,
Adam Bede, still knew his pulse a part
Of that slow heart-beat of green earth
That brings the wheat to ear, the wood to prime
Then slowly seasons to fulfilment.
Within the world of Ellastone, font to grave,
Lay all that men required to round their days,
Season on season, known but different,
Broad and narrow rings expanding to life's tree.
Power, today, switch at finger-tip,

Derives from those far steaming bobbin towers
Or more remote atomic pile,
Unseen, unheard, unknown,
Feared for its infinite potential flame.

Sun fades, distance merges earth and sky;
Thinner, colder air creeps with the shadow
Down the hill to Wootton. Rousseau, exiled,
Walking here two centuries ago,
Had these same thoughts of danger and disease
In our estrangement from the common soil,
The rhythm of its year a local pulse
Of wider amplitude than jazz-beat
Monotone that dulls the narrowing world.
Could all men come, singly and alone,
In quietness sense the magnitude of this small hill,
Power, though multiplied a million-fold,
Might serve the simpler human needs,
Descending shadow be but passing
Of a fertile cloud across the natural sun.

MAY DAY

—Ipstones

A bunch of kingcups hangs
Above each cottage door.

Children know this day, sense
The common pulse within
Themselves and springtime sap.

Age tears the calendar :
Each bunch of kingcups hangs
In witness of our years.

CONSALL FORGE

Following the pack-horse way from Belmont
Then descending by two hundred steps
To this close valley, quiet but for the sound
Of water from a weir, industry
Seems distant; yet generations back
These woods were stripped, levels reached along
The valley sides for coal and ore,
Pack-horse gave place to plateway then canal
And finally to railway line and steam

Canal and railway derelict,
We once more tread the pack-horse way
And smile to think how small the lasting worth
May be of so much toil—grass will grow again
On motorways, leaving no more trace
Than here at Consall Forge.

We who walk this valley, feeling at one
With stillness of a small green world, well know
Tomorrow's woods may hide Earth's scars;
Human hurt is seldom healed by time.

BEESTON TOR

November mist drifts unevenly—
Now impenetrable, clearing for a moment,
Silent, unpredictable, movement unfelt
Where valleys meet and air-streams eddy.
This subtle veil, moved slowly by no hand,
Magnifies the limestone cliff, making
It more vast, more sheer, with indistinctness
Yet gives clarity to the distant past
When this great tor was refuge and a living-place;
Thin mist, spiralling above a cave
High on the rock face, becomes wood-fire smoke
Of those who lived here after Roman rule.

When our precarious age disintegrates
There will be no refuge in the lonely place;
All will be wilderness, all streams be dry
As Hamps and Manifold, the air itself
Will sink in mist's contagion.

When our precarious age disintegrates
Let future time be everlasting mist
To shroud Earth's folly from the universe.

ALONG THE MANIFOLD

Fish-leap summer, shallow flashing stream,
All the water-meadows emerald,
Early green and singleness of thought
With day-dream's momentary unity
Of one small world;
Infinitude, fenced within one field,
Hangs timeless in slowly dancing air,
Sundial finger halted by rose-rimmed
Daisy or the melting buttercup
Of sun-touched gold;
A rindle from a worked-out mine
Reflecting the living light
Will not move the gnomon, neither will
The moment when the silent lark falls
Remit this spell;
There is within each seeding meadow,
Uncut as yet by the dividing
Iron of dicing personality,
A cyclic pattern of seamless days,
Cloak of childhood;
Here the floral commerce of hive bees
Obeys a final law, nectar-pull
Alone, not knowing the watershed
Parting two neighbouring narrow worlds,
Bleak moor between;
Here June's wind turns back a ladder fern,
Late ash-leaf and air-linked cirrus sky,
All many-fingered yet path-pointing
The listing wind—fern, leaf, cloud
Leading one way.

Soon, quick knowledge of the present past
Breaks sunlight;
Slowly a rainbow forms and colour,
Complementary to every mood,
Acquires significance—water

12

Is a moving mirror to the world
From spring to sea.

Leaping and leaving where the curved rocks
Fold and press their former buried stress,
Time loads mind with iron link;
Gnat-dance, morning bird-song, milking time,
Sunrise, sunset, all one life-short day,
Bud, tree-leaf, fall, water-flash then frost—
Fresh man-made detail marks each decade,
Rock-face unchanged.
Unchanged? Fluid inflexibility
Written in a cursive stratum line
Spells but gnat-dance in eternity,
And the limestone bud, now leaf, will fall
To scree, then dust.

Yet we feel ourselves immutable,
Transcending fact, beyond each premise,
Smiling as at night a pebble falls
Making the barren hill-top balder;
Cave of refuge, introspective skull,
Swallet into which live water leaps,
Leaving the slowing pulse to falter
On its sucking bed in brackishness
Until all's dry; the valley now
Is barred and pathless under ash trees
Listless with no pointing wind:
This was no leaping but straw-clutch
Past crag and narrow cavern;
Loss would have been the greater gain—
Music illumined Proserpine
But here is no sound;
No sound but thought's nailed footfall on rock,
Anxious blackbird's harsh metallic cry
At dusk; under grey ash-trunks no human voice
On this closed way,
On this track no hand-clasp traveller;

In the long parched night but nettle-sting,
Pitfall and imagined shadow,
Quest for lost river, forgotten stream.

Living, but leaving—the leap is lost
And the black hour beyond false midnight
Brings the heart-stop moment,
The brain-cease dissolution of will.
What then remains?
The footstep thread from that first meadow
Set along the valley thoughtlessly
When all pointed one way and that way
Coursing with the river in the blood
To pulse there still;
With coming light, dew films cracked rock,
Blood veins new-spread sky
Mirrored in fresh meadow pools.

Sound of water breaking with the dawn
Is Orpheus striding from the cave;
Life and love are linked
Through darkness into day.

NEAR SWINSCOE

Tread the road, near to the hedgerow verge
Where stitchwort, delicately white, more homely campion
And thrusting foxglove rise from keen-bladed grass;
Tread the road aware of beauty—
Not as those who pass,
Destroy . . . that desecrating rag
Lying, moving slowly in the wind.

Nearer, the rag becomes a bird,
Starling with broken wing, staring,
Limply fluttering; not litter,
Death—yet death is litter
Dealt with this indifference.

There was beauty in that emerald-speckled breast;
They did not see, those others
Degrading wing to rag;
They could not know,
Did not tread the road.

Lift the slowing heart-beats to the shade
And softness of the dew-damp verge;
Hand draws back, too sensitive
To reach beyond the useless thought.

Pass by, pass on the other side,
Pass with those who did not sin—
They did not see.
And feet move on, each limb thrice denying
In treason to the heart.

Returning, with tired tread at the day's end,
The way down from the rounded hill
Is dark with blood.

THE HURT OF IT

The hurt of it! Beauty's blade
Thrust in the beholder's eye, wounds
Probed green again by spring—
Yellow-green of early May growing
To duller hues of summer
When pain is stilled.

The hurt of it! Beauty's finger
Plucking each string within the heart,
Vibrant with lark-song notes
That resonate, revive remembered pain
Till summer, myriad-winged among
The trees, drowses to indifference.

The hurt of it! Beauty's fragrance
Drifting from rich lilac heads
To flash a recollection
Of one primeval May
Before the heavy incense of more sultry
Days drugs to warm sleep.

But why this hurt in beauty?
Why this twist of steel in joy?

Time? Knowledge that greenness dies,
That lark-song falls to silence,
Fragrance dissipates on careless winds?
Not this . . . not this alone:
In beauty's purest joy Time dies—
The wordless hurt remains.

Comparison? Despair
That willed creations of the mind
Can never match this unwilled force
Of sap, instinctive song?
Not this: in beauty's contemplation
Will is dead—the hurt remains.

No, here is the truth of it :
In those unmeasured moments we become
As God—comprehend opposed infinities
Whose tension gives potential power ;
Reaching to the pinnacle of joy
We sense the mirror-depth of grief—
Strings of consciousness, made taut,
Know the plangent throb of immanence.

A BOULDER

Standing on a darkly quarried hill
Once etched by ice, I passively beheld
A boulder, lopped and lying as though felled—
A lithic tree rock-seasoned to fulfil
Its sculptured destiny, unheeded till
Some deeper eye should free the form withheld
From common sight, too carelessly repelled
By seeming husk from want of sentient skill :
Knowledge, an unfeatured mound of barren fact
With many boulders mossed by grey deceit,
Awaits the scour of frozen cataract
To shape inbeing wisdom and complete
By sharp experience the life that lacked
All form and tumbled to its own defeat.

ABOVE DOVEDALE

The sun, though hidden, pillars on a wood;
Its plinth, a rounded group of April trees,
Makes firm foundation—then a sudden breeze
Dissolves their unity and each small bud
On twig and bough is seen; beyond, there stood
Unrealized hills—now their limestone screes
Are sharply crystallized, all details freeze
For one brief instant on Time's spindrift flood.
Our sight is often thus confused by near
Inconstancy, dulled by mists of urgent
Trivia until one moment rises clear
To make us for a while percipient
Of purpose in Earth's surging life; we peer
Beyond mere sight and find a testament.

WOLFSCOTE DALE

Not the lithe beauty of a rising trout,
Not curve and sparkle of clear water on the weir—
Morning light in Wolfscote Dale;
Not the quiet overture of spring,
Contentment that descends with autumn leaves,
By Drabber Tor the winter solitude:

Summer crowd! Most reared amid machines
With rivet eyes that focus narrowly
And cannot widen to embrace even this small dale;
Whose ears, dulled by modern noise, are deaf
To older sounds—water ripple, dipper's song;
Whose tattered minds, fearful of tranquillity,
Believe transistors' dead monotony is life;
Children who play on pavements, not in fields;
Lovers who walk harsh streets, not hedgerow lanes;
Men whose rhythm is mechanical, unreal.

> Office, rolling mill and loom
> Rattle round the mental bones,
> Water from the mountain spring
> Seeps between unmortared stones;
> Now these stones that formed a weir
> Tumble in disordered streams
> Tossing water where the sun
> Stabs the shadow of our dreams;
> For each dream is lived alone
> In a grey unpeopled land,
> But each crowding day is linked
> By common need—a welcome hand.

Not green perfection shielded by smooth hills,
Not limestone crag that dazzles in high sun
And dims the eye to life within the stream;
Not vacant world of superficial light
Nor brilliance of some vista in the mind
That blinds to nearer finite differences:

Summer crowd! The blur at length resolves—
Two walk slowly hand in hand, one sits alone,
Three shouting children scramble to a cave
And give new meaning to this narrow dale;
The shadow stream becomes disturbed, rocks echo,
Beauty that was readily defined is seen
A lifeless thing until the wakened heart
Pulse warmer blood, the eye regain its clarity.

LINES WRITTEN BEFORE A LONG JOURNEY

Within an hour of home, choosing the day,
Pilsbury, Crowdecote, Parkhouse Hill and Chrome,
Or, in high summer, listening to bees
Among the thyme within a garden :
There is a deepening contentment
In a near world intimately known,
Minutely different in its sun and shade—
First lamb, primrose, cuckoo, bluebells, hay,
Then blackberries and the mellow pause
Of autumn ; sap, blood, both in slow rhythm
Sinking to their rest.

Between acceptance and indifference
Is a world of movement, active
With strong tides to one or other shore ;
The simple love of small things local
Drowses to a commonplace of sleep.

Eye, teach again the mind to leap
More lightly, unburdened by mistrust ;
Thought, mingle in imagined streams ;
Heart, beat through known woods to higher hills
Then turn, walk the valley as a quest.

ON REAPSMOOR

Woman, trudging your winter road
Across a friendless moor
Coming from market, laden,
Carry your bread alone :
Knowing the wilderness
Look for no outstretched hand—
We who pass
Are not your neighbours.

RETURN IN ATOM-TIME

Beyond the childhood town
So little changed, the mingled crowd
Still patternless yet ruled by fingered time;
Beyond planned suburbs, to the wide
Moor, unhurried seasons, wordless laws
That yet remain our arbiter.

Turning, the road is vacant;
Not looked-for loneliness of lane
But emptiness of house where present
Is all past, damp air stale:
This road is dead,
Skid-marks in the dust condemn.

Mute dust, mushroomed, settled,
Indiscriminate—the road a thread
Unventured; vacant fear
Shrinks all, a fetter-creed
Of unbelief invests the town:
Dispersed, invisible the shroud.

GRADBACH HILL

Walking, alone, on this November day,
nightmare prophecy of final war
is stilled to recollection;
atomic mist shrouds all Earth's folds, on each
bruised rib grey lichen-rings reveal putrescence;
reek from sodden mountain grass
mingles with acrid fingering
of charred bilberry; four tumbled walls
remind of human fires before
the abstract conflagration, free kindled hearth
before the binding incandescent chain.

Earth has died; Evil has dissolved again
to Chaos that brief division of the second day;
the eastern law of cyclic time spins true
while western myth of history, forward thrust,
has over-reached its stroke, shattering
the elaborate temple of material power;
until the splinters of the iron altar soften
in warm rust, Chaos of this long non-solar day
shall annul known forms
and this annihilating vapour
drape a silent Earth.

Sunk on scabbed rock, where crystal still keeps
pattern to vibrate, a million beats
phase a new millenium; far below,
breaking the silence following our curse,
Black Brook soothes earth onward to the sea
whence, from equal cells untouched by pride,
new temples shall arise, sun haze fresh hills
to eyes that see beyond them
to the God who died.

NOT IN THE MORNING LIGHT

Not in the morning light—
Soon, winter makes the heart
A bloodless thing, shrunk
To a rigid head,
A tribal badge
Of close conformity.

Not in the morning joy—
Soon, memory is heavy
And too much bitterness
May flick the tongue
To a stiletto word
That makes no mark but kills.

Not in the morning act
Of praise and thankfulness,
For night continues doubt
And, though the sun ascend,
A fungus cloud remains
About the world's sick mind.

BY CASTER'S BRIDGE

Here, where two streams meet, the water moves
More quickly—dark where a pool holds back,
White over hidden rocks, onward, away,
Away from the watcher to the far sea ;
And yet the river is unchanged, ceaselessly
The same and will be when the leaves,
Now red and gold, fall from the mountain ash
And water-drops are gripped as ice where spray
Now drenches grass.

More strangely, this stream still moves towards
The plain, the sea, during blind hours of night ;
Boulders on the steep hillside, purple
In the setting sun, will stand there cold,
Uncoloured, yet not lose their essence
Though no eye can see.

Thus will be eternity :
Each drop, each crystal, cell,
Returned to the dark stream—
The stream itself
Frozen in viewless night.

BEYOND DANE COTTAGE

Under a stunted oak, sheltered by leaves
And bracken from slow rain, I look
Into a little valley—rock and stream,
Birch-tree, bilberry, gorse, nothing imposed
Except, above the further bank,
A rough stone wall that marks
The end of meadowland.

Watching the fine grey rain,
Hearing it drop from leaf to leaf
Unhurried to the draining stream,
I think of cities.
Who is nearer to the heart of things?
The many in a crowd who chatter,
Mingle, link relationships
But, webbed with triviality, fear silence?
Or those who choose to sit beneath
A stunted oak, deriving thought
From mere environment?

Grass moves; nothing seen—
A hunting vole or shrew.
What has meaning? Moment of an act
Or thought abstracted from the act?

ABOVE THE RIVER DANE

Valleys broaden, languid, to the plain,
Rivers falter, sullen, to the sea ;
Better an upland pathway firm on rock,
A little stream—the Dane,
Unfettered, free.

Flowers grown richly on a valley floor
Quickly overbloom in vain display—
Better the modest harebell on the hill,
The heather-purpled moor
Though far away.

On such a hill above the tumbling Dane
Lives one who tends with care her calves and lambs—
Better the beauty of a simple truth,
Open to wind and rain,
Than worldly shams.

EVENING ON GUN HILL

Slowly the hill-top fades—or seems to fade,
For what has substance, what is made of air
Is not dependent on a trick of light
But lives, a hill of commonplace reality
That few ascend. Experience treads
The valley road, already dark, and those
Who choose to walk that way go chilled,
Never feel the kindled glow of climbing faith—
Falling, never know themselves deceived.

Freely, the hill-top wind, fusing night and day
In measureless embrace, moves in the valley;
There it channels closely to the heart
Healing division with humility.

Blindness is the real deception.

THEE A STRANGER ?

—Cloudside

'The wind comes down the hill,
Backens things. The soil cakes dry after rain.'

Merely a statement, factual,
No shuffling of blame.

      The old man rests on his fork.

'He'd been in hospital;
There weren't no relatives. I took him in.'

Merely a statement, factual,
No self-righteous claim.

      The woman goes about her work.

FORD GREEN HALL
*(To the memory of **Raphe Sutton**, carpenter)*

Relic of a rural age, half-timbered island
Breaking through a dead-sea residue
Of crusting industry, that falsely threw
A glittering wave along the valley; sand,
A barren bed, seemed quickly fruitful, and
The humus of a thousand years, true
Tilth, a worthless mould that merely grew
The common grass without the world's command.
But now, within a card-pack house, we play
With toys and fear the universal beat
That rhythmed past and future with today,
Disunion flakes our life, with tinsel feet
We stumble, fall, become a ready prey
To atrophy—in sand there grows no wheat.

BUS RIDES

Through narcotic smoke and dirty glass
This quickly moving deck reveals
What's hidden from the street; I look
Beyond the wall and see the garden
But, where dream had made a lawn I find
A wilderness; where fancy placed a flower,
The creeping tangle of a poisoning weed:
And yet the wall of this suburban castle
Seemed to guard some treasure from the crowd.

A lifetime onward and from this high deck
Once more I move above the wall,
But now, with dream and fancy faded,
I look beyond the husk and see the house:
Already past, I see within one room
A crystal vase, within that vase a rose;
And now I know that all we see
Even from this unaccustomed plane
Is through narcotic smoke and dirty glass.

WAY TO THE SEA

Inner mountains, hidden streams, are unremembered,
Backward-trailing clouds disperse :
Only the plain, only the dusty plain
Feeding immediate needs
Has affinity with appetite ;
And the plain is but a green line
Thinning as we walk the grooved street,
Dull recollection of hedgerow holidays.
Holy? We walk forgetful through hot streets
And yet the mark made in our infancy,
Seared with the faith of centuries,
Deeply, still guides to distant steeples
Where mental peals continually cry
Along ancestral arteries.
Only the street, only the littered street
Founded on sand and flanked by little shops
Tawdry with the moment's souvenirs,
Halting the listless wind that bloweth.
Bloweth? Echo . . . Ecce Homo . . . only echoes.

A seagull gleaming high above this canyon
Glides, a trinity of head and wings,
That dazzled eyes may recognize
For one brief moment souvenirs as gaud,
And sense the murmur of an unseen wave :
The imperceptible ascent toward the far sea wall,
Made with declining day, divides the closing scene
Of this long-unacknowledged odyssey
With sword-edged shadow ;
The jetsam crowd is swallowed into palaces
Drugged with another's dreams
To wither near the never-visioned sea.

SMALL THINGS

The falling year imprints an alder tree
Bristling against impassive skies;
Upon a stunted thorn
Bright fruit is borne
On leafless branch; small things we despise
In summer mount in worth as we
Survey our winter poverty:
The ebbing tide reveals lost beauty where
It leaves a seaweed pool; curlews flock
Along an empty shore,
Forsake their summer moor
For saltings; on one rock
Grey thrift fades in mordant air—
Small things etch deeply
In a world laid bare.

WEEDS

Familiar as the bittersweet of privet flowers
In circling suburb, or smell of fresh-clipped box,
The golden glow of dandelions now richly dowers
This uncropped field and soon red-seeding docks
Will fountain from parched grass; see where low yarrow,
Some call it milfoil—meaning thousand leaves,
Already grows around a rusting harrow
And the frail wind-flower closely weaves
Eye-sounding bells about a thorn;
Groundsel in harvest-time will hold
Small misty moons aloft, breaking the dawn
For these unwondering eyes grown old.

THE *PATRIN*

Two grasses, trivial in the roadside dust,
That one day's traffic quickly blows away.

Two grasses plucked by some gypsy, deep
In wisdom gleaned along the narrow *drom*,
And plainly telling that a brother, close
To a slower pulse and not yet blind,
Passed early in the dew-light, recognized
The deceptive turning, left his mark
For those who follow sensitive to know
That each grass torn and left to die
Has individual significance.

Patrin, a trail; *drom,* a road. (Romany words)

SPRINGTIME FROST

Springtime frost killed future flowers
Yet others—there across the lawn—remain
To give their promised joy;
Untimely cold of night-long hours
Gripped this garden to destroy
Beauty, present, yet to come;
But while these buds hang blackened, those still
Keep their green, await releasing rain
To free their splendour.

Frost touched all, bowed them in the chill
Of dawn; and yet it was the needful sun,
Warming too suddenly, that charred these tender
Leaves to blackness.

Above this uncertain plain,
Beyond its bareness,
A shielding rock
Stands on an eastern hill.

SEPTEMBER MORNING

Stubble drips, condensed from night;
Memory of summer severs with the straws
Of yesterday : there will be no gleaning—
Let the dead field dry then burn, smoke drift
In slow dispersal of acridity.

Mist of the uncertain dawn,
Smoke of day's uncompromising end—
Between, far haze that cannot be resolved :
Plough to the searching touch of frost
That crumbles to renewing tilth.

WINTER LIGHT

Hollow light of winter, levelling
Each hill, brimming rivers
To the brink of disbelief,
Fades to sharper brilliance
In the freezing dark when stars
Leap, waking with staccato points :
These shake complacency, force recall—
Premonitory memory, pattern
Imposed by mind on mind beyond
The circle of the mathematically known.

Hollow night, receding dome described
About that single point, the eye, reveal
Each river as a flowing galaxy ;
Mirror near hills to show
Their final watershed.

WHERE IS THE SLEEP ?

Litter of this day is burning,
Burning down the western sky;
Late sun, red, is sinking,
Sinking in a dormant sea.

Boat, a little barque, a coracle—
Where is the shell that shrouds into the west ?
Day fades to dark, darkness into calm—
Where is the sleep that slowly drifts to rest ?

WORDS

Words are as leaves,
They shrivel, trees stand bare.

Forest wind is sibilant,
Infinitive—to fear ;
Branch snaps turbulent,
Imperative—make fall.

Will fresh sap rise, bud
New vocabularies ?
Will there be new spring vibrant
With unfaded images ?

Words are as leaves :
Leaf-mould, seeds root there.

THREE SONNETS

I

They say that there are other worlds than this
Where life may travel its conditioned road,
Though hatched irrational soon with tribal code
Then laws—most enforced by artifice;
From those worlds too some being may dismiss
To space a loaded thought that will explode
Within a kindred cell—a seed thus sowed
May only seem to float in wild caprice.
Why should this Earth alone among the spheres
Disperse its thought? The universe is named
As one, then how, with planets distant peers,
Can Earth be claimed unique? Freed minds have framed
A cosmic unity where all coheres;
Within their grasp infinity lies tamed.

II

Strange flickers of infinity have flamed
When some unbidden and unspoken thought,
Escaping free, has instantly been caught
By one I love; moments such as these have shamed
All creeping doubt and rapidly reclaimed
Those fens where too much questioning has brought
Nothing but brackish flood, leaving untaught
The truths at which analysis had aimed.
Is disembodied thought the answer then
To our far questing from this waning Earth?
The individuality of men—
By Christian creed implicit in their birth,
Their burden, immanence—is valid when
Thought is resonant with human worth.

III

If thought throughout the universe is free
To range, untrammelled by environment
And tradition's chain, can we be content
To make our trivial world epitome
Of all creation, seeing here the key
To birth, to death and all the firmament
In lifeless orbit, solving the intent
Of endless space and time's eternity ?
Yes, for this Earth is anvil where our thought
Is forged, the hammer common problems, blows
Mostly unseen of men and meaning naught
But that their iron discipline bestows
Experience, tempered and slowly wrought
To pierce beyond what little learning knows.

THE OLD SIMPLICITY

The old simplicity, living by the heart-beat day,
Is dead :
Man (mere concept of convenience)
Spiders his own web, ties down
The wings of impulse till they lose all lift
And atrophy ;
The tongue is held to rigid silences
No longer rippling with the pulse ;
Blood, that might transfuse into a darkened life,
Is drained.

The web we spin is filament of custom, rule—
As with material things, stronger
The more finely drawn until at length
We struggle meshed by unreality :
Our final cry will be unheard, soundless
In a vacuum.

Yet custom is necessity
And liberty derives from discipline,
A paradox resolved only when the bonds
Of habit and of will themselves dissolve
In love ;
Shining, the triple framework of true living
Is revealed again—verities intangible
Yet valid in a rusting world
Self-chained.

SIGNPOST

Here on No-Man's Green,
A vacuum between three backing shires,
I stand and point : thither Niddershall
And over there—you see two spires ?—
High and Nether Breen ;
Along that tangled bridle-path to Lode ;
Down there—you'd think it easiest of all
The radiating ways—I firmly state
There's No Through Road
(It serves a farm or two but then a gate
Bars progress and beyond is wilderness).

This No Man's Green? Three acres lost
And yet an immemorial meeting-place,
For these old tracks have crossed
At this fixed point since men first came this way ;
That shapeless boulder is their earliest trace,
A simple mark-stone rolled there as a guide
For simple men and still unmoved ;
That other block, now lying on its side,
Accurately socketed and grooved,
Was base of butter-cross—or so men say
Although in all my time I've never seen
A butter-pot on No Man's Green !
Butter-cross or no it served its day
As landmark when few travellers could read
But all knew piety.
And last myself descended from a line
Of wooden posts ; we stand our seventy years
Then fall and rot. But men need
Guidance, men demand a sign :
We know the way, we three—
Boulder there so close to earth it cannot stray ;
That remnant of a cross, lost even to memory . . .
Of men . . . marking an earthly pilgrimage ;
And I who stand awhile, then back to mould.
We know, we three—

Instinct, symbol and the written word
Here at this cross-roads, age on age,
And we have told
All travellers—some heard.
But we, like one brought here
And buried stake-through-heart by night,
Remain ; far and near,
The foul road and the fair, depth, height,
We know them all ; and yet we may
Not move but only mark the way.

KNOWN—UNKNOWN

Rock, crag, Earth's skull
Known by lens and X-ray beam;
Soil, silt, Earth's skin,
Analyzed to micron grain;
Grass, tree, Earth's hair,
Numbered, classified and named;
Atom tagged, star docketed,
Computed by electron brain.

These myriad facts all known
And yet
Another's mind unknown
Except
By Mind, by Mind alone.

CREEDS

To stand on rock, high above cities,
Approaching pathless emptiness,
Comes near to knowledge.

To lie on earth, level with low grass
Among highways of abundant life,
Comes nearer to understanding.

THE WOODCARVER

No torn horizon, tugging mountain peak,
Underfoot no trampled flower, mute question,
But midway pause, balanced on the year's turning,
Urgency of spring stilled, fetter-chain
Of winter not yet fastened on the heart;
Is this the moment—free from will,
A canvas world of warm tranquillity ?

The moment past, will demands creation;
Chisel, brush or pen must capture,
Pin the undefined though to realize
Mean lose. Only the untrue is lost,
There is a residue of gold within the palm
Of understanding.

Beyond the anonymity of cities,
Beyond the animal reality of fields,
There is woodland—open, not dense forest,
Play of light on leaves, not fir-wood shuttering :
There, within the cabin of his thoughts,
A Woodcarver keeps chastely trimmed
A symmetry of light, a form remembered
At the unrevealing hour of dawn,
Dissolving in the shimmering noon.
In green simplicity the Craftsman
Listens to a clear insistent voice :

    'Truth hovers in the eye—must be revealed :
    Create ! Then will others comprehend
    The power of beauty for eternal good.'

The still voice commands fulfilment,
Vision must be realized ; but this final
Consummation demands more than common wood,
A tree most perfect.

The Woodcarver had known this tree since infancy—
Broad oak, trunk craggy, dark column

Dividing into fingers like a wrist,
Bared in winter—a prophetic hand.
Felled in full maturity, the tree
Had seven years seasoned ; now, the destined time,
From the trunk a single billet, true-grained,
Free from any knot ; last, with rule and square,
Proportions humanly defined to frame
Perfection.

> 'Create ! Then will others comprehend
> The power of beauty for eternal good.'

The maiden form within his mind guides
His untroubled skill in firmly balanced line ;
As though he pared a sheath from his own thought
The chisel-point releases meaning
From linked material cells—tree and man
Derived alike from water, earth and air.
Bright diffuseness hardens to the light
On polished wood ; eye sees reflection
Of intelligence that scans all things
Externally and quickly learns beauty
Of repeated pattern, veined beech leaves,
Seasonal across the broad bole
Year-dial rings ; beauty of surface
Colour or the covering of frost on grass,
Beauty ripple-winged in butterfly
And gliding bird. The intellectual eye
Has focused these and all things tangible
To budding loveliness, not of a woman
Known and deeply loved, but abstract
Thought of mirrored maidenhood.

The carving now stands central—more remote ;
Far from human traffic, the ideal
Is fragile as a dream ; imagination
Stripped to naked truth may prove a lie :

Beauty seen within the mind—
Violet, beech tree, crimson sky,
These we mould to match our thought;
Violet never was unkind,
Beech tree never was untrue,
And we know the cloud to be
Grey within the factual eye.

Beauty dressed in human form
Assumes the blemishes of sin,
Wears the jewelled clasp of pride,
Nourishes the envious worm,
Breathes corroding words of hate
Thus we learn that lips can smile
Though jealous fires leap within.

The carving stands remote, the Carver far from joy;
Taken from his treasury of thought, graven,
Wood becomes the idol of his solitude—
The worshipper must learn, not here, alone
In green woodland, but lonely in grey streets
Where charity is loaded with men's sin :
The tree from which true carving grows,
Though planted in a garden, withers
Until watered by the bloody sweat
Of Man's divinity.

Older, in these streets, the Woodcarver,
Seeking to convince that truth is single,
Abstract essence of all beauty seen,
Ultimately learns that myriad greys
Of multitudinous living form a wider
Spectrum than the narrow greens of solitude.
Native thought, not tempered by experience,
Gave form to an ideal; within a city
Where broken facts replace a seamless faith,
Form has no significance. He sees
Majestic buildings, mounting stone on stone,
Where other eyes see only offices ;

The miracle of an ascending spire
Where others cannot follow; he feels
The breathless thronging of great thoroughfares,
Unbreathing silence in small sanctuaries,
The sweep of an embracing colonnade,
Unplanned grace within a market-square.
There he shows his carving: few pause,
Some glance with empty eye, some jeer.
In this city of excessive wealth
Beauty is of little worth—
The purity of an ideal
Conceived by solitary questioning.

> For this is truth: the knotted, warped, rough, cracked!
> Truth is greed, envy, lust, avarice!
> Blot and scar—carve these, common truths
> For all the multitude, things they know;
> Seek out the hollow tree twisted by disease,
> Deformed by storm-lash, whip of the sterile moor.
> Knots—carve knots to eyes, each knot a leering eye!
> Crooked grain . . . body crooked, hunched in hate,
> Wealds stark, warped with pain; carve these
> Truths of tarnished streets.

Granite paving stones thrust hard against
The iron heel; dark temple walls
Stand gaunt as sepulchres; a blackened tree,
Roots strangled, chokes in burdened air,
Forcing the unseasoned eye to ask:

> 'How can beauty be released from rough
> Complexity where seasons clashed?
> Where sap froze in summer drought, then split,
> Warmed and warped by winter plenitude?
> Beauty cannot dwell in chaos!'

Yet from chaos came this world.

Walk further on the granite stones, beyond
The temple walls, palace, prison, offices,

Past hovels, hidden slums; here stands
A medieval hospital, warm,
Neighbourly, nodding on the teeming street.
Unwilled, the Woodcarver has vision
Of a fine facade of weathered oak
Taken as it came from the forest,
Carved by comprehending fellowship
To motley of a market crowd—
Warped ones laughing with split sides, gnarled ones
Resting there content; men, women, some grotesque,
Some beautiful, each billet taken whole:

Carved into fat men and lean,
Chiselled to varlets and cheats,
Some of them foul and unclean—
All of them drawn from the streets.

Many are twisted and split,
Many are cross-grained and old,
Some had been thrown in the pit—
Fallen to rot in the mould.

Heat of the day made them crack,
Hatred of men made them warp,
They needed the love that men lack
But witness to hands that knew hope.

In this unconscious masterpiece above a door
Where outcasts once found refuge, the Woodcarver
Learns wider truth: that mere perfection
Following the outline of an image
In the mind, never warms the heart;
To carve that all will comprehend,
The drying sap must flow again as blood,
Chisel touch the inner vein; beauty
Must be found in truths of the working day,
Of scorching noon, cold waking hours of night.

The blackened tree becomes a silhouette
Against grey sky above the temple walls,
Its agonizing limbs more meaningful
Than smooth dome or symmetry of towers;
Here the paving stones are worn, trodden
By silent feet since the tree's planting, granite
Softened, hate transformed by understanding.

The city now has lost its anonymity,
The market crowd resolves;
Only the perfect carving
Lacks a name.

55

PRINTED AT SEVENOAKS BY KNOLE PARK PRESS LTD.